Go2FAS Growing Threat Series

COLLEGE BOUND READINESS TRAINING

*Training that saves lives -
Don't be a target, Don't be a victim*

Go2FAS Growing Threat Series

COLLEGE BOUND READINESS TRAINING

Training that saves lives - Don't be a target, Don't be a victim

At Form A Strategy (F.A.S.), we offer a series of training venues on our Growing Threat Series. I wrote these workbooks as part of the training I have been teaching since 1985 as a Martial Arts, Krav Maga, and Defense Instructor. As a veteran, I have traveled the world and have both witnessed and have been engaged in multiple levels of violence. At F.A.S., our mission is to deliver our experiences and offer training that builds confidence while enhancing survivability.

Here are the most recent updated training workbook titles in my Growing Threat Series.

1. **Situational Awareness**
2. **Psychology Of Violence**
3. **Active Shooter Response**
4. **Home Invasion**
5. **Carjacking**
6. **College Bound Readiness**
7. **Workplace Violence**
8. **Surviving Civil Unrest**
9. **Severe Weather Survival**
10. **Surviving The Apocalypse**
11. **The Dark Truth About Sex Trafficking**
12. **Kidnapping And Abduction**
13. **Dry Fire to Live Fire**
14. **Gun And Knife Defense**

Chapter 1 -
Threat Overview

For many young people going to college represents the most exciting time of their lives. It represents freedom from the restraints of living at home under parents' rules. It's a time to explore themselves and their dreams and discover things about themselves that they didn't know while getting a wonderful education.

But it also represents a great deal of trepidation, stress, and fear as well. For many of those young people, college represents freedom and the first time living away from home, but also far from home. College may be in a different city or an entirely different state, and so as they think about it, living that far from the safety net of their parents doesn't sound as appealing as it once did. The reality is whether you watch the news or stay up to date online, Active Shooters, Abductions, Sex Trafficking, Sexual Assault, Rape, Violent Crimes, and so many other criminal events that occur on campus.

But these fears are perfectly normal and to be expected, and to one degree or another, they happen to everyone, whether it's college-bound readiness or not. However, with a. few short training sessions, one can prepare themselves for attending college.

But we understand that's a part of life and a part of growing up. It's their first real experience in the adult world and leaving that of children behind.

But despite whatever sense of maturity they think they have, they're still young people. And they aren't as mature as they think, aren't as wise, and aren't as keen to the dangers they'll face in the real world. And some of these dangers are far beyond their meager ability as young people to truly grasp and absorb. One can wrap their heads around the occasional mugging or theft, but sex trafficking, hard drug addiction, rape, and murder are unthinkable. And that's precisely why they should be thought about. Because they represent an ugly reality, many don't want to consider or face.

Then there are other illnesses and sicknesses young people are exposed to because of the nature of campuses. These things may not seem as horrible as rape and murder, but they can also leave a young person scarred for life, debilitated, or damaged for the rest of their lives because of diseases and sickness.

In short, there are many threats to fall prey to for the unprepared, and that's precisely what we don't want you to be. College should be an exciting time for young people, and they should, in an ideal world, be able to explore that world in a relatively safe and secure environment.

The confidence comes in the form of feeling safe and secure and knowing how to respond.

<u>**Growing Threat Series**</u>

Violent Encounters - Don't be a target, Don't be a victim

College Bound Readiness Training Workshop

1. **De-escalation Strategies**

    a) Verbal
    b) Threat

2. **G.E.A.R.**

3. Guard

    Guard - Situational awareness. Be aware of your surroundings.

    a) Situational Awareness Signs
    b) Evacuation Measures
    c) Avoidance Measures
    d) Physical Encounter
       - Open Hand
       - Edged Weapon
       - Gun Defense
       - Weapons Of Opportunity
    e) Resistance Measures

4. Evacuate

    Evacuate - Time is not on your side. Evacuate the area.

    a) Situational Awareness Signs
    b) Evacuation Measures
    c) Avoidance Measures
    d) Physical Encounter
       - Open Hand
       - Edged Weapon
       - Gun Defense

- Weapons Of Opportunity
  e) Resistance Measures

5. **A**void

   Avoid - If one cannot evacuate, take avoidance measures.

   a) Situational Awareness Signs
   b) Evacuation Measures
   c) Avoidance Measures
   d) Physical Encounter
      - Open Hand
      - Edged Weapon
      - Gun Defense
      - Weapons Of Opportunity
   e) Resistance Measures

6. **R**esist

   Resist - When confronted as a last resort, resist.

   a) Situational Awareness Signs
   b) Evacuation Measures
   c) Avoidance Measures
   d) Physical Encounter
      - Open Hand
      - Edged Weapon
      - Gun Defense
      - Weapons Of Opportunity
   e) Resistance Measures

Now, let's discuss some of the basic training scenarios and how the G.E.A.R. will apply to them.

1. Car

Training Scenarios:
Each training scenario offers training in the following areas.

A. Basic

Automobile is safely secured and cannot be started.

I.   Open hand
II. Knife defense
- Walking to and from the car
- Trunk and hatchback
- Ingress
- Egress
- Driver's seat
- Front passengers' seat
- Rear seats

Notes:

B. Advanced

Training Scenarios:

Automobile is safely secured and cannot be started until range scenario.

    I.   Open hand

  II.   Knife defense

 III.   Weapons of opportunity

 IV.   Gun Defense

  V.   Permit Carrier

- Walking to and from the car
- Trunk and hatchback
- Ingress
- Egress
- Driver's seat
- Front passengers' seat
- Rear seats
- Range scenario

Notes:

____

____

____

____

2. Parking Lot

Training Scenarios:

Each training scenario offers training in the following areas.

A. Basic

Training Scenarios:

Basic training scenarios that are proven to save lives.

I. Open hand
II. Knife defense
- Movement through a parking lot
- Around vehicles
- Large crowds
- Day & Night

Notes:

____

____

____

____

B. Advanced

Training Scenarios:

Advanced training scenarios.

I. Open hand
II. Knife defense
III. Weapons of opportunity
IV. Gun Defense
V. Permit Carrier
- Movement through a parking lot

- Around vehicles
- Large crowds
- Day & Night
- Range scenario

Notes:

____

____

____

____

3. On-Campus Grounds Outside (day and night)

Training Scenarios:

Each training scenario offers training in the following areas.

A. Basic

Training Scenarios:

Basic training scenarios that are proven to save lives.

I. Open hand
II. Knife defense

- Campus grounds
- Walking alone
- Walking in groups
- Large gatherings

Notes:

____

____

B. Advanced

Training Scenarios:
Advanced training scenarios.

    I.   Open hand
   II.   Knife defense
  III.   Weapons of opportunity
  IV.   Gun Defense
   V.   Permit Carrier

- Campus grounds
- Walking alone
- Walking in groups
- Large gatherings
- Social media settings
- Being followed
- Day & Night
- Range scenario

Notes:

4. Dorm | Residence Halls

Training Scenarios:
Each training scenario offers training in the following areas.

A. Basic

Training Scenarios:
Basic training scenarios that are proven to save lives.

I.   Open hand
II.   Knife defense
- Secure room and valuables
- By yourself
- With others
- Forced entry
- Active shooter threat

Notes:

____

____

____

____

B. Advanced

Training Scenarios:
Advanced training scenarios.

I.   Open hand
II.   Knife defense
III.   Weapons of opportunity
IV.   Gun Defense
V.   Permit Carrier
- Secure room and valuables
- By yourself
- With others
- Everyday living

- Forced entry
- Active shooter threat

Notes:

____

____

____

____

5. On-Campus Grounds Inside

Training Scenarios:

Each training scenario offers training in the following areas.

A. Basic

Training Scenarios:

Basic training scenarios that are proven to save lives.

I. Open hand
II. Knife defense
- Protection from identity theft
- A.T.M.'s
- Violent encounter
- Active shooter threat

Notes:

____

____

____

B. Advanced

Training Scenarios:
Advanced training scenarios.

    I.   Open hand
    II.   Knife defense
    III.   Weapons of opportunity
    IV.   Gun Defense
    V.   Permit Carrier

- Protection from identity theft
- A.T.M.'s
- Computer scams
- Violent encounter
- Active shooter threat

Notes:

____

____

____

6. Off-Campus

Training Scenarios:
Each training scenario offers training in the following areas.

A. Basic

Training Scenarios:
Basic training scenarios that are proven to save lives.

    I.   Open hand
    II.   Knife defense

- Con artists
- Living off-campus
- Road rage
- Public transportation
- Neighborhood safety
- Active shooter threat

Notes:

____

____

____

____

B. Advanced

Training Scenarios:
Advanced training scenarios.

I. Open hand
II. Knife defense
III. Weapons of opportunity
IV. Gun Defense
V. Permit Carrier

- Con artists
- Living off-campus
- Road rage
- Public transportation
- Neighborhood safety
- Active shooter threat
- Home invasion

Notes:

Additional Training Drills & Notes:

Chapter 2 - Knowledge

The college-bound readiness course considers various threats and their impact on any student on and off-campus.

The number one threat students must contend with at college is stress and fear. Many of these are associated with the unknown factors while attending school. Stress over the pore pressures the unrealistic goals is becoming increasingly common and opens the door to numerous other threats. But stress alone itself can be a killer, literally. Suicides have increased as students are unable to cope with unrealistic expectations placed on them either by themselves or by others, or both. Then there is prescription drug abuse and addiction. As students try to cope with stress and other threats, they resort to pills to keep them going. This again opens them up to numerous other threats, but the drug abuse alone can be a killer.

Alcohol-related injuries are also chief among the sometimes more minor threats they can face, but yet again, they are related to other threats and can open the door to more. A young person is injured and begins taking pain pills to try and manage. One can see where that becomes a life-threatening problem if it isn't properly dealt with. Illness and disease are also increasing threats when students are exposed to bugs from places their bodies aren't familiar with and aren't conditioned to process or deal with.

Theft is yet another, and the dangers of fire on campuses are still another threat.

And all of these represent only the more minor threats. Rape, murder, Active shooters, abduction, dorm room violence, and sex trafficking are threats that must be acknowledged and considered when going to college.

One of the ways to combat these dangers is to research and reference which colleges are most dangerous or pose the most threats according to where the young person is considering attending is among the first steps we can take to protect our young people. Then talking with them and acknowledging these threats is perhaps the most useful avenue of protection. Educating them and encouraging them to seriously consider these threats and ways and means by which they can avoid them are among the most valuable assets you can supply them with.

Remember, training is a key element before or during ones attending college.

And finally, instilling in them the value of remaining aware of danger, remaining aware of the threats they will face is something that will aid them on their way and offer you a means of being with them anywhere they go if they remember the things, you've taught them.

You can also introduce them to the steps of G.E.A.R. as it could apply to their attending college-bound readiness.

Chapter 3 - G.E.A.R.®

With every course taught, the G.E.A.R.® concept I developed over the years is taught as a

4 - step system to give direction. G.E.A.R.® training at F.A.S. hardwires the ability to Form A Strategy in a world full of chaos.

Guard - Situational awareness. Be aware of your surroundings.
Evacuate - Time is not on your side. Evacuate the area.
Avoid - If one cannot evacuate, take avoidance measures.
Resist - When confronted as a last resort, resist.

GUARD

In the Growing Threat series of books, GUARD has always signaled situational awareness. And with college-bound readiness, situational awareness is still employed directly as a constantly functioning passive skill. We want our young people to enjoy the adventure of going away and exploring college. But we also want them aware of the potential threats they may face from virtually any quarter. Situational awareness will save lives in a world full of active shooter events to violence on campus that isn't always in the news.

And with the passive deployment of situational awareness, there is no reason they cannot satisfy both simultaneously. Most people see situational awareness merely means paying attention and listening to our instincts when they challenge us against a decision we may make. However, training scenarios help align situational awareness with the ability to Form A Strategy (F.A.S.). By no means does this mean we intend for them to be constantly paranoid to unrealistic threats around every corner. It simply means we want them to be aware of the presence of those threats, and just as they deploy situational awareness to the dangers of driving in traffic, so do they deploy situational awareness to the dangers of navigating their way through college.

Situational Awareness...

From on and off-campus dorms, parking lots, and parties to walking through a park or in a mall, this skill set we call guard saves lives.

Wherever possible, we want them to form close bonds with people or friends they can trust. The more people that bond together and form cohesive trustworthy relationships, the more they build a potential safety net for themselves and each other, which can aid them and support them where we as parents may not always be so readily available. Remaining situationally aware means taking sensible precautions and being prepared for any such eventuality of threat. Just as one buckles a seatbelt and remains situationally aware in traffic, they take similar precautions in their daily lives on campus. It operates passively and doesn't interfere with anything they are doing. It simply alerts them to the possibility of the presence of a threat if and when it should arise. And this allows them the time and opportunity to avoid those dangers and take the necessary steps to see to their safety. In virtually every other trade, profession, or career pursuit, people take necessary and sensible precautions against the various threats they may face in those instances. Instill in your young people that it only makes the most rudimentary sense that they would do the same in their pursuit of the college experience.

EVACUATE

We practice pre-planned evacuation routes for other threat situations which emerge in the immediate term. But there is absolutely no reason the same can't be done for threat situations young people might find themselves in during college. They should be taught that if they find themselves in any situation in which they feel threatened, they should evacuate, they should leave, or exit that situation. With proper training and planning, a route will already have been thought of prior to an event.

Just as immediate threats have a hot zone of danger in a concentric circle around them, so do threat situations have the same in the longer term. For instance, if they are at a party in which they feel distinctly uncomfortable, perhaps they sense something is off, or for that matter, have no rational reason, but still feel threatened, they should evacuate, they should leave the party. It's that simple. But they must also be taught the signs, body language, and what to look for in multiple scenarios. They have this step instilled in them that it's ok to leave if they feel threatened. They are under no obligation to prove anything to anyone. And that it's truly better to be safe than sorry. It bears reminding that law enforcement frequently speaks of situations they have seen in which someone was hurt, injured, or killed. And in looking back, clearly saw instances in which situational awareness and the employment of evacuation could have saved injury or could have saved lives. There is no shame in walking away from situations we aren't comfortable with. Pre-planning is essential, from going to a party to being caught in an active shooter event.

AVOID

Avoidance is the ability to use one's awareness of the surroundings, the environment, and the situation to avoid a negative or dangerous experience. In many cases, seen quite often in the news, avoidance measures utilize barriers for protection.

In this sense, it is encouraging and teaching our young people that if they do find themselves in a situation in which they feel threatened, not only should they evacuate and leave, but they should also avoid falling prey to it. In the G.E.A.R. scenario, avoidance measures are utilized during evacuation routes.

Many times, it's as simple as knowing what to use to avoid danger while evacuating.

Additionally, the lessons we've gone over before in actually being threatened still hold as much credence here as there. If they are physically under assault, they are to create distance by evacuating. Along the evacuation route, one will need to know what can be utilized to be heard and seen, to avoid physical contact to avoid having a weapon utilized against you or another.

This applies as much to the long term as the short term. Creating distance, concealment, cover, and other strategies and tactics are utilized to keep safe under the **A**void training G.E.A.R. It is a way of avoiding danger and conflict. And it should be practiced anytime they feel threatened.

RESIST

Resistance takes many forms, and a young person must be taught that it can be resorted to and should when deemed necessary. They are not victims, and they do not have to be victims. They have a right to safety and security wherever they may be. And that includes college. It must bear reminding to us and to young people that college is supposed to be a place of critical thinking. A place where critical thought is practiced and encouraged. And that must include the safety and sanctity of their minds and bodies. Resistance, and the practice of it, is critical thinking. It is the ability to defy being a victim. And the stronger their minds are, the stronger their character will be, and so will their ability to successfully resist threats and danger and navigate the college experience.

Data has shown us that if being abducted and you cannot evacuate or avoid being abducted, resist prior to being taken. **R**esist is the last resort whether in an active shooter situation, rape, abduction, carjacking, or robbery. In some cases, within the G.E.A.R.® training, it's the first action to take as it may have been a surprise attack.

In this course, we cover basic to advanced scenarios, and each one has various resistance strategies and tactics.

Chapter 4 - Scenario

While our Growing Threat series normally incorporates a scenario in which the reader might find themselves encountering a given threat, in this book, we wanted to try something different. We wanted to show the steps of G.E.A.R. can be applied even to a wider scope of potential threats, and it remains viable in all of them. As we have covered in many other threat situations, a person can employ the skill sets of guard, evacuate, avoid, and resist to protect themselves, and the same remains true of the broad spectrum of threats they might encounter. If a young person finds themselves facing a threat of any kind, they can still employ these steps to help guide them away from it. If a student is facing mounting stress to the point that it is becoming a tangible threat, they would employ the steps in this way. Guard means remaining situationally aware, and the fact that they've acknowledged that the stress is becoming a threat to their health and well-being means that they've successfully employed guard and that they've become aware of the threat itself and are initiating steps to do something about it. Next, they would employ the steps of evacuation and avoid and create distance or remove themselves from the threat. Finally, they would take the step of resistance and create ways in which they can defend themselves from the effects of stress that are threatening them. The point is that they have identified a threat, and they have initiated steps to create distance, guard themselves against it and take a preemptive move to do something about it. They aren't simply allowing themselves to fall victim and suffer consequences when they might not have had to in the first place.

Guard means to remain situationally aware of your surroundings. Wherever you may be, or whatever those surroundings may be, you are remaining aware of threats to your health and well-being.

Evacuation means to use a pre-planned escape route to remove yourself from danger. If there is a fire, you get out of the building; if there is a temptation to resort to prescription pills you haven't been prescribed, you remove yourself from that threat. If it's an active shooter on campus, you may be able to safely evacuate.

Avoid means to create distance and interrupt the chain of events that lead to victimization by using your training and the environment for cover and concealment.

Resist means that you physically fend off an attacker, and it also means that you actively resist anything that threatens you. If stress is mounting and overwhelming, you seek ways to reduce it, to remove it, and to restore a necessary balance in your daily life that allows you to function and overcome that obstacle. It means the opposite of allowing yourself to fall victim.

All the steps of G.E.A.R.® can be employed both passively and actively to see that a young person successfully navigates their college experience and exercises their right to safety and security as well as prosperity.

Utilizing G.E.A.R.® means you are utilizing and practicing a certain state of mind. That of being free and unrestrained. It means you are refusing to be a victim and that you are remaining accountable for your actions, as well as inactions. It means that you acknowledge that there are threats existent out there but that you can assess them, evacuate, avoid, and resist them. You don't have to be a victim, and you refuse to be.

Chapter 5 - Summary

In nearly every case of threat, one the chief elements faced is isolation. Isolation means that the young person feels alone or is alone and thus unable to cope with whatever threat they are being faced with. It means that their ability to employ the steps of G.E.A.R.® might be hampered, and their ability to protect or defend themselves is lessened. It doesn't have to be that way. By teaching them and encouraging them to form and create trustful bonds with friends and family as well as staff, they can better protect themselves, they can feel more confident, and they can be more proactive in enabling themselves to adequately protect and defend themselves from any threat they might be faced with.

And in virtually every threat situation, the presence of allies could make a significant difference. Teach them and encourage them to watch out for each other, combine their abilities of situational awareness and employ those for their own greater good.

In a former Growing Threat series book, we asked the question of what it would be like, what it could potentially look like if everyone in society employed situational awareness passively whenever they were in public. Virtually any threat could be identified before it could become too great. Evacuation, Avoidance, and Resistance could then be employed actively against that threat. The very same principle applies here. If we encourage and teach young people to look out for each other, practice situational awareness and, pre-plan escape routes, pre-plan a process for identifying and mitigating threats, then their ability to pursue happiness, freedom, and dreams would be magnificently enhanced.

If you have a young person going to college soon, or if you are attending college now, take the time to talk with them. Look over the potential colleges they may attend. Consider the safety implications of each of them. What are the dangers or threats present there? Is stress endemic? Are drugs and alcohol a major issue? Have there been reports of sex trafficking, disappearances, rapes, or murder? How have the staff responded to these threats? How adequate has law enforcement been in investigating these things? What safeguards and measures are in place to mitigate the damage of these crimes? Have there been instances of rape being covered up by the athletic program because it brings in too much revenue, and protecting a star athlete has been more important than protecting a young girl and honoring her right to safety and security and her access to justice? Look closely at whatever college is being considered and have your young person discuss them with you, find out how they feel and where they stand. While you can't force a young person to take security seriously, you can make your best efforts to prepare them. And that's not all you can do; seek training such as the Form A Strategy College Bound Readiness courses.

Talk with your young person about how they would respond to instances, and help them create pre-planned escape routes in various scenarios. What would they do if someone was trying to accost them, rob them, or force them into a bedroom or van? How would they cope with mounting stress? How would they respond to an invitation to take drugs, resort to prescription pills to deal with stress, or some other malady? How would they respond to an active shooter, how would they respond to any number of scenarios? The point here is obviously not to enhance their fear or fill them with dread or encourage them to be paranoid. It is rather to make them aware of potential dangers that do exist and encourage them to practice the passive deployment of situational awareness and simply take it seriously.

If they can take their fun and games seriously, they can take their safety at least equally seriously. It's as simple as that. And if they employ the steps of G.E.A.R.®, They can ensure a greater chance of living the life and experiencing college the way they imagine, in as much safety and security as can be devised.

www.ingramcontent.com/pod-product-compliance
Lightning Source LLC
Chambersburg PA
CBHW061322250726
48653CB00002B/1003